Lire à petits pas Niveau

Méthode Montessori pour apprendre à lire : du mot au livre

French English German Spanish - Slovak

milk | lait

Lait

leche | mlieko

The baby is drinking milk.

---

hoe | houe

houe

azada | motyka

Use a hoe in the garden.

---

score | but

But

puntuación | skóre

What was the final score?

children   les enfants

les enfants

niños   deti

Four children sang.

---

leg   jambe

jambe

pierna   noha

My leg is feeling better.

---

father   père

père

papá   ocko

He is a nice father.

example

exemple

exemple

ejemplo

príklad

This is an example of a bird.

---

men

hommes

Hommes

hombres

muži

The men are arguing.

---

cow

vache

vache

vaca

krava

The cow is standing up.

day	journée

journée

día	deň

This day is the 30th.

watch	l'horloge

l'horloge

reloj	hodiny

My watch is ticking.

nose	nez

nez

nariz	nos

My nose is running.

kitty

minou

minou

gatito

mačiatko

I like my kitty.

water

l'eau

l'eau

agua

voda

He is drinking water.

conditions

conditions

conditions

condiciones

podmienky

What are the weather conditions.

rose	rose

Rose

rosa	ruže

Thank you for the rose.

birthday	anniversaire

anniversaire

cumpleaños	narodeniny

Today is my birthday.

time	temps

temps

hora	čas

He is telling the time.

fish

poisson

poisson

pez

ryby

There are two fish.

---

cat

chat

chat

gato

mačka

That cat is adorable.

---

flower

fleur

fleur

flor

kvetina

She is holding a flower.

table

table

table

mesa

stôl

There is a toy on the table.

pig

porc

porc

cerdo

prasa

She is lying on the pig.

tree

arbre

arbre

árbol

strom

She is sitting under a tree.

| wind | vent |

vent

| viento | vietor |

The wind blows the leaves.

| school | école |

école

| colegio | školské |

They are going to school.

| boat | bateau |

bateau

| barco | čln |

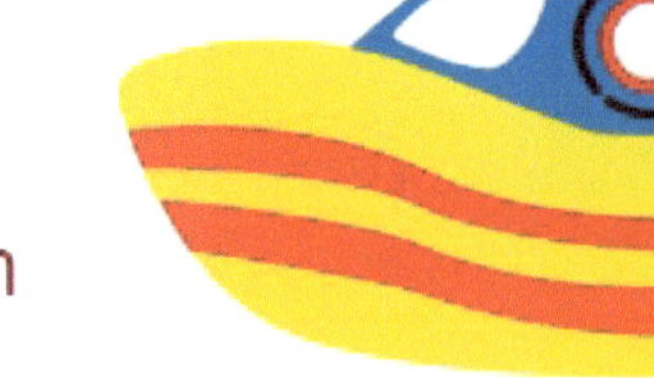

The boat is sailing.

street   rue

rue

calle   pouličné

They walk across the street.

---

column   colonne

colonne

columna   stĺp

Did you read the newspaper column?

---

seat   siège

siège

asiento   sedlo

The girls took a seat in the sand.

nuit

night

nuit

noche

nočné

nuit

We sleep at night.

Nom

name

nom

nombre

názov

Nom

My name is Joe.

colline

hill

colline

colina

kopec

colline

The house is on the hill.

bell   cloche

cloche

campana   zvon

I hear the bell ringing!

---

oxygen   oxygène

oxygène

oxígeno   kyslík

What is the symbol for oxygen?

O_2

---

children   les enfants

les enfants

niños   deti

The children are playing.

game

jeu

Jeu

juegos

hry

What game is it?

duck

canard

canard

pato

kačica

The duck is swimming.

France

france

France

francia

Francúzsko

Have you ever been to France?

food   aliments

aliments

comida   jedlo

They made a lot of food.

---

toy   jouet

jouet

juguete   hračka

He has a whole box of toys.

---

garden   jardin

jardin

jardín   záhradné

They are going to the garden.

rope   corde

corde

cuerda   lano

Do you have any rope?

---

morning   matin

Matin

mañana   dopoludnia

I wake up in the morning.

---

bread   pain

pain

un pan   chlieb

She is baking some bread.

head   tête

tête

cabeza   hlava

She has a hat on her head.

---

floor   sol

sol

suelo   podlaha

The girl sits on the floor.

---

brother   frère

frère

hermano   brat

They are brothers.

shoe   chaussure

chaussure

zapato   střevíc

I have new shoes.

---

grass   herbe

herbe

césped   tráva

The goat is eating the grass.

---

apple   pomme

Pomme

manzana   jablko

Apples are a popular fruit.

chart   graphique

graphique

gráfico   graf

What does your medical chart say?

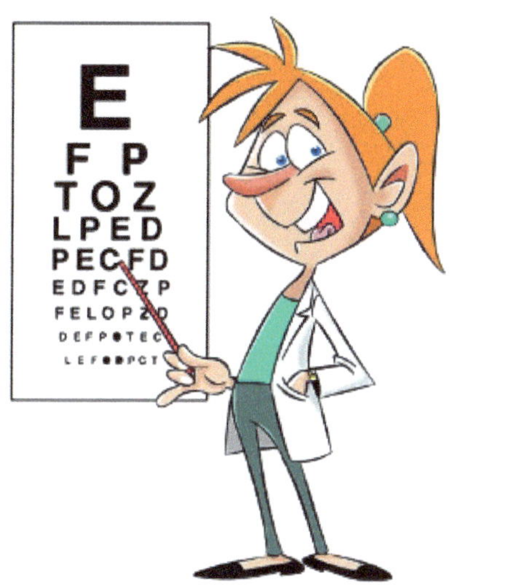

four   quatre

quatre

cuatro   štyri

There were four of them.

home   maison

maison

casa   Domov

He drew a picture of his home.

mother   mère

mère

madre   matka

My mother loves me.

baby   bébé

bébé

bebé   dieťa

The baby is crawling.

letter   alphabet

alphabet

alfabeto   abeceda

Learn English letters is fun.

dog
chien

chien

perro
pes

The dog wants to eat sweets.

office
bureau

Bureau

oficina
kancelária

Do you need any office supplies?

snow
neige

neige

nieve
sneh

I have fun in the snow.

farm   ferme

ferme

granja   farma

The farm has lots of animals.

---

window   fenêtre

fenêtre

ventana   okno

The window is open.

---

idea   idée

idée

idea   nápad

I have an idea!

ring   bague

bague

anillo   krúžok

The bird is holding a ring.

---

nest   nid

nid

nido   hniezdo

The bird has a nest.

---

girl   fille

fille

niña   dievča

The girl is pretty.

bed   lit

lit

cama   posteľ

We all share three beds.

---

city   ville

ville

ciudad   veľkomesto

He worked in the city.

---

bird   oiseau

oiseau

pájaro   vták

The bird is dancing happily.

cotton   coton

coton

algodón   bavlna

A q-tip is made of cotton.

---

top   haut

Haut

tapas   top

We like to play with tops.

---

page   page

page

página   strana

Please turn the page.

company   compagnie

compagnie

empresa   spoločnosť

What company do you work for?

chicken   poulet

poulet

pollo   kura

The chicken is laying eggs.

wood   bois

bois

madera   drevo

He plays with wooden blocks

horse   cheval

cheval

caballo   kôň

The horse is galloping.

---

rain   pluie

pluie

lluvia   dážď

We love the rain!

---

family   famille

famille

familia   rodina

How big is your family?

money   argent

argent

dinero   peniaze

I save money in my piggy bank.

song   chanson

chanson

canciones   piesne

She is singing a song.

man   homme

homme

hombre   muž

This man is my dad.

coat   manteau

manteau

saco   kabát

She is wearing her coat.

Greek   grec

grec

griego   grécky

Have you ever had Greek food?

---

eye   œil

œil

ojo   očné

He is closing his eyes.

feet   pieds

pieds

pies   chodidlá

His feet are swollen.

---

picture   image

image

imagen   obrázok

He is taking some pictures.

---

car   voiture

voiture

coche   auto

My car is fast

box   boîte

boîte

caja   box

The box is full of clothes.

---

rabbit   lapin

lapin

conejo   králik

The rabbit wants to play.

---

egg   oeuf

Oeuf

huevo   vajíčko

The bunny has many eggs.

corn	blé

blé

maíz	kukurica

I grow corn in the garden.

ball	balle

Balle

pelota	lopta

He is bouncing the ball.

door	porte

porte

puerta	dvere

He is knocking on the door.

thing   chose

chose

cosa   vec

I am thinking of many things.

chair   chaises

chaises

sillas   stoličky

He is sitting on the chair.

stick   bâton

bâton

palo   palica

He is playing sticks.

fire   feu

Feu

fuego   požiarne

Fire is hot.

squirrel   écureuil

écureuil

ardilla   veverička

The squirrel is on the tree.

doll   poupée

poupée

muñeca   bábika

She is hugging her doll.

hand   main

main

mano   ručné

You should wash your hands.

---

ground   sol

sol

suelo   prízemný

It plays a trick on the ground.

---

boy   garçon

garçon

chico   chlapec

The boy is eating dinner.

farmer   fermier

fermier

agricultor   krajan

The farmer had a farm.

place   endroit

endroit

sitio   miesto

This is my favorite place.

house   maison

maison

casa   dom

We live in the same house.

bear   ours

ours

oso   medveď

The bear likes to eat honey.

---

paper   papier

papier

papel   papier

I like to color on paper.

---

cake   gâteau

gâteau

pastel   torta

The cake is white and pink.

sun   soleil

Soleil

dom   slnko

The sun is very bright.

---

gun   pistolet

pistolet

pistola   zbrane

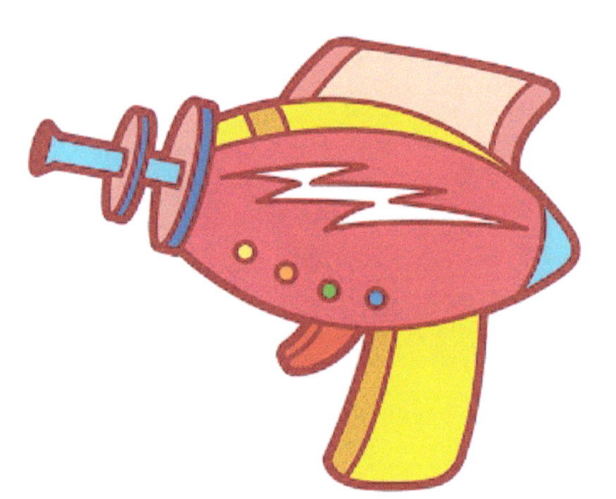

We played with a water gun.

---

sheep   mouton

mouton

oveja   ovce

The sheep have fluffy wool.

fresh | frais

Frais

fresco | čerstvý

All the fruit is fresh.

---

face | visage

visage

cara | tvár

They were at the face painting booth.

---

way | façon

façon

camino | spôsob

They find a way back home.

church   église

église

iglesia   cirkevné

Did you go to church?

---

party   fête

fête

fiesta   večierok

I love to go to parties.

---

goodbye   au revoir

Au revoir

adiós   Zbohom

The bear is saying goodbye.

seed — la graine

la graine

semilla — semienko

We will plant the seeds.

---

sister — sœur

sœur

hermana — sestra

She is my sister.

---

robin — robin

Robin

robin — červienka

The robin is helping Santa.